# 125 Quotes for Whacking Weasels

*Centuries of*
*Wisdom, Motivation and Snappy Comebacks*
*from The Cranky Middle Manager Show™*

W. Wayne Turmel

125 Quotes for Whacking Weasels



ISBN 978-09820377-0-6

To Joan, The Duchess

All my love, always.
You may quote me.

I'm not quite sure when I realized that repeating things people smarter than me said made me look more intelligent, but I can sure tell you when I realized it would help at work.

If you read my first book, *A Philistine's Journal, an Average Guy Tackles the Classics*, you can skip this paragraph. Of course, if you've read this, it's too late so just stick with me and it will be over soon enough. It's not like there are enough of you to worry about.

I was getting yet another gust of hot air from yet another sales person complaining about a looming deadline. Rather than repeat for the fifth time that their order came in about three weeks after the cutoff date, I leaned back in my chair, looked around the conference table and said…

"As Robert Browning said:
*'June reared that bunch of flowers you carry*
*from seeds of April's planting'* "

A hush fell over the room. Some were amazed that I knew who Robert Browning even was… most had no clue themselves but weren't inclined to expose their ignorance (a good quote can glue a mouth shut faster than anything except peanut butter).

Still, it was much more eloquent than, "These things take time" and if someone that smart said they take time, well who were they to argue?

I knew I was on to something. Whenever I sent out a memo to my team after that, I'd include a quote. They might ignore me – after all I'm just the boss and not all that bright – but they shrug off Leonardo da Vinci at their peril.

memorize tons of quotes.

Today Google makes that skill seem quaint, but, just like making your own pasta, people are far more impressed with the effort than the final results warrant. Bless their gullible little hearts.

Maybe more importantly, whenever I ask myself, "Is it just me?" I find that no, it's been like that for thousands of years. Not a solution, perhaps, but definitely a comfort.

Michel de Montaigne, who you'll meet in these pages, is one of my favorite sources for quotes. As a businessman and bureaucrat, he had a pretty keen eye for human behavior. He put it this way,

> *"... The firmest and most general ideas I have are those which have been born with me. They are naturally and wholly mine... since then I have established and fortified them by the authority of others and the sound arguments of the ancients with whom I found my judgment in agreement. These men have given me a firmer grip on my ideas and a fuller enjoyment and possession of them."*

In other words, if they agree with what I'm thinking, they are brilliant sages and since they agree with what I'm thinking, I must be right. If they don't, they're just a bunch of old, dead, white guys who aren't relevant to today's business environment. THAT, my friends is a win-win outcome.

Since starting 'The Cranky Middle Manager Show™' podcast in May of 2005, each show has contained a quotation from someone long dead but knew the human condition all too well.

It started as a way of establishing my own credibility with a world-wide audience that had no idea who I was. If they

enjoyed the quotes as much as anything I had to say. A lesser man would be dismayed by that, but since you'd be hard pressed to find a lesser man, I was thrilled.

I went out of my way to avoid the run-of-the mill things you'd find on break room walls and on coffee mugs. "There's no 'I' in team…," for example. Well as one former employer told me, "there's no 'U' either, take your stuff and go."

Some quotes you can use ironically – like the Roman general you'll meet who refused to accept new ideas for weapons since everything that could be invented had been.

Others are designed to make you feel better about your circumstances. If misery loves company, this is a Middle Management festival.

Good people have faced long odds since we crawled out of the primordial ooze; you're not alone by a long shot.

I have felt obliged to add my two cents (and at the current value of the American Dollar it's worth even less than usual) to each quote. Hopefully this adds value. If not, the words of dozens of people way smarter than me stand on their own and even my snarky comments can't detract from their worth.

What should happen, of course, is that you read the quote and then think about it for a while. Some you'll agree with, some will resonate right away and some you'll shrug and move on. That's as it should be. The ones that stick with you stick with you because you need them.

When I find a good quote, I'll often print it up and hang it in my office. Sometimes it's for my own inspiration; mostly it's to inspire conversation with the people who come in.

I'll never forget when I wrote the Latin words "Ut biberent, quoniam esse nollent" on a sheet of paper and hung it over my desk. It inevitably inspired the question, "What's that mean?"

everyone can stick to.

It sure beat the hell out of one more memo about Key Performance Indicators and ignoring the project update memos.

Of course these words were written a long time ago. Way too many of them assume "Men" means people in general (write your own joke there) and it's hard sometimes to prove that somebody said what they were quoted as saying.

When you are in doubt as to who said it, let me give you the failsafe… Samuel Johnson. He's the greatest glory hog in the history of the English Language. When you own the newspaper you can claim credit for anything in it and that's his secret. And again, no one has actually finished any of his books since 1834 so no one will call you on it.

Oh, and if it sounds vaguely Asiatic, you can always claim Confucius said it, but you run the risk of sounding like you got it from a fortune cookie.

It is, of course, impossible to attribute good quotes to him if they contain the words e-mail, computer or Jobs. The modern equivalent of Samuel Johnson is Seth Godin, If he didn't say it, someone linking to him did and that's close enough for our purposes.

Keep these words alive – pass them along, use them with your team, argue them out on long nights in the lounge at the sales meeting. That's what they're there for.

Here's to keeping the weasels at bay.

Enjoy.

---

Try using this one to talk some sense into your IT people....

***"A tool is but an extension of a man's hand, and a machine is but a complex tool. And he that invents a machine augments the power of a man and the well-being of mankind."***

**Henry Ward Beecher**

Okay, so a machine is supposed to augment the power of a man and the well-being of mankind. Someone tell that to our crack IT staff. They've given us tools to span the globe in seconds but can't get my printer to talk to my laptop without printing in what I'm pretty sure is Sanskrit.... And when I try to send it to another printer it says... "Dave? What are you doing Dave?"

We don't need cool, we just need functional, gang. Cool comes second.

***"… in life, take advice rather from actors, who choose not the best roles, but those most suited to them."***

**Cicero**

Cicero had maybe the biggest ego ever to walk the earth. He had a way of annoying people to the point where he was eventually assassinated – which is kind of the ultimate performance review. Even GE hasn't gone there… yet. If Jack Welch had stuck around a little longer instead of that wimp Immelt, who knows….

***"Because your own strength is unequal to the task, do not assume that it is beyond the powers of man; but if anything is within the powers and province of man, believe that it is within your own compass also."***

**Marcus Aurelius**

Dang, huh? Just because you don't think you can do it doesn't mean it can't be done by someone… and if someone else can do it, then you can, too. Let's see someone put *that* on a poster with an eagle on it and hang it in the break room.

Here's a little tidbit. There were basically two schools of philosophy in Greece – Epicureans and Stoics. The Epicureans basically believed in "eat drink and be merry, for tomorrow we die." The Stoics believed "Go ahead, eat, drink and be merry, 'cause tomorrow you'll die, probably from something you ate or drank."

***"To accuse others for one's own misfortunes is a sign of want of education. To accuse oneself shows that one's education has begun. To accuse neither oneself nor others shows that one's education is complete."***

**Epictetus**

Epictetus was obviously a stoic. Life is hard, deal with it and stop whining. He'd have made a great middle manager, although unlike me, he wouldn't have had to send out complaining memos about the staff wearing sandals on casual Friday.

Of course, it was Greece, everyone was wearing sandals, and a chiton looks a lot better than the Hawaiian shirts that show up on the Sales team from time to time.

***"Whatever is done skillfully appears to be done with ease; and art, when it is once matured to habit, vanishes from observation. We are therefore more powerfully excited to emulation by those who have attained the highest degree of excellence, and whom we therefore with least reason hope to equal."***

**Samuel Johnson (really)**

When using quotes in an attempt to look smarter, you'll get extra points for attributing them correctly. This has two advantages – it adds power to the quote and gives you a psychological advantage over the person you're arguing with – after all what are the odds they've read Johnson? No, they'll smile and nod sagely, as if they have heard of him (yes he's a real person – Google it) and as any negotiator will tell you, getting the other party to start with agreement is the first step to victory.

***"The Crowd will follow a leader who marches 20 paces ahead of them... but if he is a thousand paces ahead of them, they will neither see nor follow him."***

**George Brandes**

"No, tell you what, we'll get your team to use the new system first and then the rest of us will join you once it's tested".... Hands up anyone who's fallen for that one... twice.

***"Our plans miscarry because they have no aim. When a man does not know what harbor he is making for, no wind is the right wind."***

**Roman Senator Seneca**

When it comes to the latest flavor of the month from HR, it's not the wind that causes plans to fail, it's the hot air….

***"Observe always that everything is the result of a change, and get used to thinking that there is nothing Nature loves so well as to change existing forms and to make new ones like them."***

**Marcus Aurelius**

Millions of people bought *Who Moved My Cheese* to learn to cope with change. Fans of the show will know this is not my favorite book. I know where my cheese is, I'm just lactose intolerant. The cheese is right where I left it; it's my JOB that's gone to Bucharest.

This quote is from Alfred Lord Tennyson who was more of the flashy McKinsey consultant type than a middle manager, still....

***"Because right is right, to follow right***
***Were wisdom in the scorn of consequence."***

**Alfred Lord Tennyson**

In other words, sometimes you gotta suck it up and do what's right, and hang the consequences. Here's a performance metric for you. If that doesn't sound like something you've said at least once a week during your career you're not taking care of business.

***"Our minds are like our stomachs; they are whetted by the change of their food, and variety supplies both with fresh appetite."***

**Marcus Fabius Quintilian**

Besides being absolutely true, I love this quote because Marcus Fabius Quintilian is simply one of my favorite names to drop. Say it with a pseudo-European accent.... Marcus... Fabius... Quintilian.... Don't you feel smarter already?

***"'Tis not how long we have to live,
But how much pleasure is to come
That real wisdom would enquire
Would Oracles proclaim our doom."***

**British Poet John Thelwall**

When was the last time you asked an interviewer, "How much fun will I have on this job?" Pleasure, you remember… like fun… digging what you do? I'm not talking fun like the company picnic – which is usually anything but. Nothing that fraught with politics and potential for career-ending behavior should hide under the guise of innocent frolic.

I once spent three weeks on an analysis project just for beating my boss and his brat in a three-legged race. He claimed it was a "delegated task."

Delegated: from the Latin meaning "Paybacks are hell."

***"All progress is based on a universal innate desire of every organism to live beyond its income."***

**Samuel Butler**

Yeah, that's exactly why you became a manager… remember?

***"We learn wisdom from failure much more than success. We often discover what will do by finding out what will not do; and probably he who never made a mistake never made a discovery."***

**Samuel Smiles**

Samuel Smiles, near as I can tell, was the first person to write a book simply called, *Self Help*. Now, of course, there are entire sections in bookstores and libraries with that title. Did he ever see one penny of it? Of course not.

Guess what he discovered the hard way is, have a good lawyer. That makes the quote all the more poignant, no?

***"It is of great use to the sailor to know the length of his line, though he cannot with it fathom all the depths of the ocean. It is well he knows that it is long enough to reach the bottom, at such places as are necessary to direct his voyage, and caution him against running upon shoals that may ruin him."***

**John Locke**

Know your resources and your limits. Of course, as my wife says, it's not the length of your line… but I think she's just being kind.

Did I say that out loud?

***"Human misery must somewhere have a stop – there is no wind that ALWAYS blows a storm."***

**Greek Playwright Euripides**

Really, it will end sometime. Of course HOW it will end is another story. It depends if you're an optimist or a pessimist.

If you're an optimist, this is a comfort.

If you're a pessimist, you would like some estimate of the end date. Remember every job that doesn't end in unemployment ends in death.

***"Consider the little mouse, how sagacious an animal it is which never trusts its life to one hole only." ****

**Roman Playwright Plautus**

Do you really think you'll never have to look for another job in your lifetime? Network like crazy and keep that resume handy and updated.

*Please note, this is career advice, NOT marital advice. 'Nough said.

***"By three methods we may learn wisdom: First, by reflection, which is noblest. Second, by imitation, which is the easiest; and third, by experience which is the bitterest."***

**Confucius**

Yes, there really was a Confucius, and yes, he did say a lot of smart things, although in many ways he's just the Chinese Samuel Johnson; when you don't know who to attribute the quote to, give it to him. Let's face it, no one is that smart all the time.

Of course no one wrote down the STUPID things he said so we'll have to take his word for it.

***"Innovators and men of genius have almost always been regarded as fools at the beginning (and very often at the end) of their careers."***

**Fyodor Dostoyevsky**

This is a comfort in two ways:

1) If you really are a genius, you're in good company.
2) If you really are an idiot, you can delude yourself that you're a genius.

Either way, don't you feel better?

***"Curiosity is one of the permanent and certain characteristics of a vigorous mind."***

**Samuel Johnson (or so we're told)**

That's especially true when getting orders from your boss. I mean, aren't you just a little bit curious what they were smoking when they came up with this year's marketing budget?

When you stop wondering why and just accept it, it's all over.

***"Forward, the Light Brigade!,***
***Was there a man dismay'd?***
***Not tho' the soldier knew***
***Someone had blunder'd***
***Their's not to make reply,***
***Their's not to reason why,***
***Their's but to do and die:***
***Into the valley of Death***
***Rode the six hundred"***

**Alfred Lord Tennyson**

Stop and read it again:

1) Everyone knew someone had screwed up but they marched anyway.
2) It's do AND die, not do OR die. They knew what was coming.

This is a warning, not a training tool.

***"It is not always by plugging away at a difficulty and sticking at it that one overcomes it; but, rather, often by working on the one next to it. Certain people and certain things require to be approached on an angle."***

**British Poet and Essayist Matthew Arnold**

If at first you don't succeed, try and try again. Then take a break and try something else for a while. What are you, a moron? Give it a rest, already.

***"An invincible determination can accomplish almost anything and in this lies the great distinction between great men and little men."***

**English Churchman Thomas Fuller**

Fuller knew a little about his subject. He had a heck of a job to do. While the English court of the 1600s was in rebellion against the King he sided with the Crown, which didn't make him the most popular kid in class.

At the same time the Royalists suspected him because his preaching was so calm and reasonable. Instead of pounding the pulpit and sending the bad guys screaming to Hades, Hell or where it is bad Englishmen go (maybe it was Australia) he was a smart guy who tended not to yell even in the most serious of circumstances.

Note, he did not believe in reform, since "Only the Supreme Power may initiate reform." He failed his Six Sigma certification as a result.

***"Those who never retract their opinion love themselves more than they love the truth."***

**French Writer Joseph Joubert**

… and way more than they love their middle management jobs. Retracting opinions is a core competency for those of us who want to stay employed.

***"No one has yet computed how many imaginary triumphs are quietly celebrated by people each year to keep up their courage."***

**Greek Poet Athenaeus**

Come on, we all do it. Here's how pathetic I am. I'll write stuff into my "To Do" list that I've already done just so I can check it off.

Yeah, like you've never done it.

***"He who labors diligently need never despair, for all things are accomplished by diligence and labor...."***

**Greek Playwright Menander**

... which is easy to say when you're a mediocre playwright with really well-connected friends.

By the way, Menander drowned in his own bathtub, so maybe it should have read "all things are accomplished by diligence, labor and actually coming up for air" (which is actually a metaphor that works on multiple levels if you think about it).

***"What are fears but voices airy?***
***Whispering harm where harm is not.***
***And deluding the unwary***
***Till the fatal bolt is shot!"***

**English Poet William Wordsworth**

It's probably all in your head. Unless you get called by the nice lady from HR. Then be afraid, be very afraid.

***"I also lay aside all ideas of any new works or engines of war, the invention of which has reached its limit and in which I see no hope for further improvement."***

**Sextus Julius Frontinus, Roman Praetor of Britain**

He said this, by the way, in the Year of Our Lord 80. Yeah, once they invented the Gladius, that was pretty much the outer limits of technology. Where else was there to go?

I give this to you as inspiration for when the weasels at work throw up roadblocks and won't give your ideas the time of day. Tack it up on your wall, write it where they can see it.

Chin up little buckaroos, 'twas ever thus.

***"Be fit for more than the thing you are now doing. Let everyone know that you have a reserve in yourself; that you have more power than you are now using. If you are not too large for the place you occupy, you are too small for it."***

**U.S. President James Garfield**

This is great advice – it's how you get on the boss's radar screen and grow your career.

Now, someone more cynical than I would point out that Garfield is primarily famous for getting shot and killed just 100 days into his term. Being too large for the place you occupy makes you a pretty good target, apparently, but I don't think that's what he meant.

***"Perseverance is more prevailing than violence; and many things which cannot be overcome when they are together, yield themselves up when taken little by little."***

**Plutarch**

The first rule of project management, process management and eating elephants is the same thing: one bite at a time.

When I'm feeling overwhelmed by the task at hand, it helps if I take it in tiny steps. Removing my hands from the throat of the person who brought me the news is usually the first one.

***"Once you make a decision, the universe conspires to make it happen."***

**Ralph Waldo Emerson**

… except with CRM implementations. Then all bets are off. Otherwise the universe is on your side.

***"When you are inspired by some great purpose, some extraordinary project, all your thoughts break their bonds: your mind transcends limitations, your consciousness expands in every direction, and talents become alive, and you discover yourself to be a greater person by far than you ever dreamed yourself to be."***

**Yogi Patanjali**

This is seldom true, by the way, when next year's sales quotas are announced.

***"Natural Ability without Education has more often attained to glory and virtue than Education without Natural Ability."***

**Cicero**

Listeners to the show know that I don't have a four-year degree, just an Associate's degree from the BC Institute of Technology, which may as well be Hogworts for all any college in the U.S. will acknowledge it.

Natural Ability, of course, is not a section on most resumes so seldom gets past the nice lady in HR. How are you spotting it on your team?

***"With regard to excellence, it is not enough to know, but we must try to have and use it."***

**Aristotle**

The problem with high standards is that you run out of excuse for not reaching them day in and day out. If you have the metrics, you have to reach them. That's what we do.

I know you know, and you know that I know you know.... But it is still a bear.

***"All truth passes through three stages… first it's ridiculed, secondly it's violently opposed, third it's accepted as self-evident."***

**Arthur Schopenhauer**

Sadly, this sounds like the hiring decision process every time I've gotten a job. What's he doing here… like hell he's working here… yeah, the kid was alright.

Remember this next time you catch yourself saying something won't work.

***"Keep five yards from a carriage, ten yards from a horse and thirty yards from an elephant – but the distance you should keep from a wicked man cannot be measured."***

**Anonymous Indian Proverb**

We don't know who said this; even Samuel Johnson couldn't take credit, since his knowledge of elephants was extremely limited. We also know it wasn't a graduate of the Indian Institute of Technology, because not only could they tell you how to measure the distance, but could give you the number accurate to six decimal places.

It's still pretty good advice – just avoid the weasels when you can – especially at the annual sales meeting.

***"The expectations of life depend upon diligence; the mechanic that would perfect his work must first sharpen his tools."***

**Confucius**

Sharpen the tools… where have we heard that before? Oh yeah, 2,000 years later Steven Covey would call it "Sharpening the Saw" and make millions. What have we learned then?

1) Good advice is still good advice.
2) All of us complaining about the Chinese pilfering our intellectual property might want to chill out.

***"We uniformly applaud what is right and condemn what is wrong – when it costs us nothing but the sentiment."***

**English Writer William Hazlitt**

A bit of an object lesson here. Hazlitt was known for being a bit of a hard case. As with many people who set high standards for the rest of us, he kind of tripped over them himself. He had an affair with his housekeeper which ultimately the right wing press used to attack him. Smart , tough but done in by an affair with an employee…. Sounds like CEO material to me.

***"Watch a man in times of adversity to discover what kind of man he is; for then at last words of truth are drawn from the depths of his heart, and the mask is torn off."***

**Lucretius**

You think you know your boss until the network goes down and she still has something to tell you… then we'll see how that communication plan really works.

***"Trust men, and they will be true to you; treat them greatly and they will show themselves great."***

**Ralph Waldo Emerson**

But wait, there's more. Assume they can't do anything without you and you'll be proven right. Congratulations, you're now indispensable. Good luck taking that vacation.

***"There are two ways of establishing our reputation; to be praised by honest men, and to be abused by rogues."***

**Charles Caleb Colton**

Bear in mind, Colton's own reputation was colorful. He was one of those guys who could be either brilliant (writer, churchman) or a complete idiot (gambler, spendthrift). He finally killed himself rather than face an operation that would have easily saved his life.

Two words Chuck… risk assessment.

***"If your actions inspire others to dream more, do more and become more, you are a leader."***

**John Quincy Adams**

Here's my theory, there are "big L" Leaders. They are proper nouns… it's in their job description. Your boss is a Leader. Then there are "small l" leaders. Might not be part of the job description, just what they do.

Remembers leaders lead but aren't necessarily Leaders. Leaders, on the other hand, are not always leaders and God knows they don't all know how to lead.

Got that?

***"There is no duty we so underrate as the duty of being happy. By being happy we sow anonymous benefits upon the world."***

**Robert Louis Stevenson**

Our duty to be happy? Hmmm, I'm checking my performance review and don't see that box. Wouldn't it be cool if someone put THAT as a core competency?

***"If nations truly want peace, they should avoid the pin-pricks that precede the cannon shots."***

**Napoleon Bonaparte**

Who knows more about starting fights than someone really good at finishing them?

What does this have to do with the workplace? Well, blow-ups and simmering grudges at work frequently start with little things, like not respecting people's property and taking that yogurt in the break room refrigerator. Do you think it just arrived there by miracle – some kind of "Immaculate Dairy Delivery"? Of course it belonged to someone… like me for instance…. Just as a hypothetical example.

Baked goods, on the other hand, are fair game. Everyone knows that.

***"We are reformers in spring and summer; in autumn and winter, we stand by the old; reformers in the morning, conservers at night."***

**Ralph Waldo Emerson**

Ahhhh the impetuousness of youth. Remember when you were the one who thought everything needed to be changed right now? Some of it still does.

***"Obstacles cannot crush me. Every obstacle yields to stern resolve. He who is fixed to a star does not change his mind."***

**Leonardo Da Vinci**

OOOOOOkay. I can't decide if this is the most inspiring thing I've ever heard… or the megalomaniacal ravings of a sales manager 40% over quota and refusing to listen to "those morons in Marketing" ever again.

***"The distance is nothing, it's the first step that costs."***

**Mme Marie de Deffand**

I know you've probably never heard of her, but she was one of the great letter writers of all time. Her point is still valid, though. There are more ways to communicate than ever before with your team, it just takes a little effort and thought.

Would you still think that email was so important if you had to write it using a goose feather?

New and more convenient isn't always better.

***"How can one learn to know oneself? Never by introspection, rather by action. Try to do your duty, and you will know right away what you are like."***

**Wolfgang von Goethe**

There comes a time when you have to stop thinking about it and just do it. Or better yet, send an intern. Call it delegation. Works for me.

***"Have the courage to face a difficulty, lest it kick you harder than you bargained for."***

**Polish King Stanislaus I**

Every time you think you had it bad, imagine being the Polish King in the 18th Century: "The Russians are coming! No, wait… the Germans… Sorry, the French…." It all culminated in getting beat by the Swedes. That's a bad day at work.

By the way, remember this at budget time… face up to the bean counters or calmly accept the ridiculously low number you'll have to work with.

***"It is almost as difficult to keep a first class person in a fourth class job, as it is to keep a fourth class person in a first class job."***

**Alexandre Dumas**

Of course, he said this in French, but I grew up in Western Canada and unless it's on the side of a cereal box I'd have no idea what he's saying.

This one I understand. Boy, do I understand it.

***"Nearly all men can stand adversity, but if you want to test a man's character, give him power."***

**Abraham Lincoln**

A little tip for our friends in HR: If someone is the first to apply for a management job, they should probably never be allowed to have it.

***"Everything that irritates us about others can lead us to an understanding of ourselves."***

**Carl Jung**

Assuming, of course, you come to that kind of understanding before you snap and not after the trial.

Yeah, it's been that kind of week.

***"The strongest is never strong enough to be always the master, unless he transforms his strength into right, and obedience into duty."***

**Jean Jacques Rousseau**

Are you strong enough NOT to have to always be the master? You don't want people following you because they have to… although, admit it, once in a while would be nice.

***"The winds and waves are always on the side of the ablest navigators…."***

**Edward Gibbon**

…and of those weasels in Sales. It's always nice weather for the Annual Sales Meeting, have you noticed?

Who do they know with that kind of pull?

***"Whenever a man does a thoroughly stupid thing, it's always from the noblest motives."***

**Oscar Wilde**

Of course, you have to give major props to whoever convinced them something that bone-headed was a noble idea in the first place. That's someone you want on your side.

***"What will not ambition and revenge descend to? Who aspires must down as low as high he soared."***

**John Milton**

Milton was blind and cranky when he wrote this.

Basically he was no big believer in personal development...If he were in HR he'd hire out of grad school and not bother training the masses. A recruiter's dream.

***"Dwell not upon thy weariness, thy strength shall be according to thy desire."***

**Old Arab Saying**
**(although Samuel Johnson tried to take credit)**

If you want it badly enough, suck it up and try again, you'll make it. Except the employee of the month award, that always goes to someone in Admin.

***"Silence is the best tactic for him who distrusts himself."***

**Francois la Rouchefoucauld**

The 21st Century corollary to this rule: Not hiring that cute intern is the best tactic for him whose wife distrusts him. Trust me on this.

***"No act of kindness, no matter how small, is ever wasted."***

**Aesop (yes that Aesop)**

Irony alert! The man who wrote these well-meaning words was killed by an angry mob for reasons that have never been made clear.

I don't know what that means but do something nice for someone today just to be safe.

***"Nowadays most people die of a sort of creeping common sense, and discover when it is too late that the only things one never regrets are one's mistakes."***

**Oscar Wilde**

When is the last time you did something truly risky at work?

Holiday parties don't count. Seriously, don't even think about it. Go home before you do something you'll regret.

***"First, say to yourself what you would be; and then do what you have to do."***

**Epictetus**

It's not that tough in theory. You want to be a good manager? Then you do what good managers do. There are plenty of books and training programs, get on it.

Of course chess is simple in theory too, the castles go one way, the horsies go another… what's the problem?

***"It is not by muscle, speed or physical dexterity that great things are achieved, but by reflection, force of character and judgment."***

**Cicero**

There is such a thing as being too eloquent for your own good. When Cicero was eventually killed by his political enemies, Marc Antony's wife took his severed head and repeatedly stabbed his tongue with a hairpin as revenge against his eloquence. Worst I ever got was "needs improvement."

Some things ARE better now.

***"Resolve to edge in a little reading every day, if it is but a single sentence. If you gain fifteen minutes a day, it will make itself felt by the end of the year."***

**American Educator Horace Mann**

If you've gotten this far, you're done for the day – take a break. I won't tell.

***"Conversation becomes intolerable when you are with men whose brain is full of boxes where everything is stowed away in order and nothing external can enter. Let us bear hospitable hearts and minds."***

**Joseph Joubert**

Have you ever tried to talk to someone who thinks they know everything about a subject? Yeah, so do the people who work for me – or so I've been told. Repeatedly.

***"Facts are stubborn things, but statistics are much more pliable."***

**Mark Twain**

Learning the fine art of using statistics to make a business case is a crucial skill for a middle manager and one that's often overlooked.

Senior Management wants to know you can make a business case for the unreasonable demands you're making – especially if you're in a non-financial or engineering role.

An HR person who can use numbers is like a tall blonde who speaks Mandarin – a source of fascination and fear for everyone and has unlimited potential.

Your team just wants to know there's some reason for the idiotic thing you're asking them to do.

Everyone's happy.

***"A horse never runs so fast as when it has other horses to catch up and outpace...."***

**Roman Poet Ovid**

Except when I have money riding on it. Then it breaks down around the quarter pole.

***"On action alone be thy interest,***
***Never on its fruits.***
***Let not the fruits of action be thy motive,***
***Nor be thy attachment to inaction."***

**From the Bhagavad Gita**

Who am I to argue with centuries of wisdom? Sometimes we need to just do the job because it needs to be done and we don't know what will happen.

Still, "do the task and don't worry your pretty little head about the results" is pretty much how we wound up with our company's T and E policy.

We really need vending machine receipts?

In duplicate?

***"Be not arrogant because of that which you know; deal with the ignorant as with the learned; for the barriers of art are not closed, no artist being in possession of the perfection to which he should aspire."***

**Egyptian Grand Vizier Ptah Hotep**

This is doubly impressive advice when you realize this is a guy who helped build the Great Pyramids and served a god directly. Taking the time to listen to the help and learn when you can simply have them mummified or fed to the alligators takes discipline.

I don't have nearly that much power and sometimes I don't listen worth a darn.

***"Resistance to tyranny is obedience to God."***

**Thomas Jefferson**

God doesn't work for Accounts Payable. Just photocopy the receipts and send them in.

***"A leader is a dealer in hope."***

**Napoleon Bonaparte**

This has been my mantra through every major re-org. There's always hope… I mean it has to work this time, right?

***"Let us rise up and be thankful, for if we didn't learn a lot today, at least we learned a little, and if we didn't learn a little, at least we didn't get sick, and if we got sick, at least we didn't die; so let us all be thankful."***

**Prince Gauddamma Siddharta (Buddha)**

Yeah, but not exactly a stretch goal is it?

***"Take a rest… the field that has been rested gives beautiful crops."***

**Ovid**

Let me put it as simply as I can. Step away from the Blackberry and no one gets hurt.

***"You can't escape the responsibility of tomorrow by evading it today."***

**Abraham Lincoln**

But you can skip out early on Friday to beat traffic.

***"To change your mind and to follow him who sets you right is to be nonetheless the free agent that you were before."***

**Marcus Aurelius**

A lot of us assume leadership means leading the pack, but we learn from others – there's no shame in following someone if you know they're right.

***"… and in today already walks tomorrow."***

**Samuel Taylor Coleridge**

As our guest, the futurist Joel Barker said, "Those who say something can't be done should get out of the way of those who are already doing it."

Keep your eyes open, the answers are out there, usually in the head of someone making less money than you.

***"Strategy without tactics is the slowest route to victory. Tactics without strategy is the noise before defeat."***

**Sun Tzu**

I've been to that meeting.

***"Look to make your course regular, that men may know beforehand what to expect."***

**Francis Bacon**

This is not permission to just keep doing what you're doing and never get better.

The difference between consistency and "the same old thing" is whether they like what you're doing to start with. If they expect fairness and thoughfulness you're good. If they expect you to suck as badly as you did yesterday, you have work to do.

***"I have observed that in comedies the best actor plays the droll, while some scrub rogue is made the fine gentleman or hero. Thus it is in the farce of life. Wise men spend their time in mirth; it is only fools who are serious."***

**Viscount Henry St. John**

If you've read this far you probably agree that truth and humor are not mutually exclusive. You know that wise-ass comment the sales guy made the other day? There might be truth in it.

Or he might be a pompous windbag who's been drinking his expense account again. Still, it probably bears examination.

***"It is not because things are difficult that we do not dare; it is because we do not dare that things are difficult."***

**Seneca**

Get started on that project that's staring you in the face and you'll probably see it's not as hard as you thought.

Except SAP installations. They always suck. But they didn't have those in ancient Rome, so Seneca can be forgiven for being overly optimistic.

***"Times of great calamity and confusion have been productive for the greatest minds. The purest ore is produced from the hottest furnace. The brightest thunder-bolt is elicited from the darkest storm."***

**Charles Caleb Colton**

If you want people to change their opinion of you immediately, print this quote and hang it over your cubicle. When people come in they think two things:

1) Does she really think she's the brightest bolt in the storm? Maybe we've underestimated her resilience and she's more impressive than we thought.
2) Are things that bad? Maybe we'd better take another look at the situation.

Either way they'll leave you alone.

***"Adventure is just bad planning."***

**Polar Explorer Roald Amundsen**

Let's face it, trekking to either Pole pretty much makes you an expert in project management.

Here's a metric for you. You know a plan has gone amiss when you hear yourself ask, "What wine goes with Husky?"

***"To travel hopefully is a better thing than to arrive, and the true success is to labor."***

**Robert Louis Stevenson**

This quote is best used during project status meetings to justify scope creep.

It will buy you an extra week but will only work once.

***"If you would understand anything, observe its beginning and its development."***

**Aristotle**

As screwed up as things are, they got this way because someone thought it was the solution to an earlier problem. Find THAT problem and you'll know what the hell they were thinking.

***"It is a sign of contraction of the mind when it is content, or of weariness. A spirited mind never stops within itself; it is always aspiring and going beyond its strength."***

**Michele de Montaigne**

Remember this when you're staring at that hotel room ceiling at 2 in the morning and can't sleep. You aren't going crazy, you're just aspiring.

***"Attempt easy tasks as if they were difficult, and difficult as if they were easy; in the one case that confidence may not fall asleep, in the other that it may not be dismayed."***

**Balthasar Gracian**

This will also give you plenty of cushion in the project timeline if you play your cards right.

***"It's by perseverance alone that the snail reached the ark…."***

**Charles Haddon Spurgeon**

I've felt like this after some meetings. Left a trail, too, on one ugly occasion, but I don't want to talk about it.

***"If you do not change direction, you may end up where you are heading."***

**Lao Tzu**

Depending on the kind of day you're having at work, this is either encouragement or a dire warning. I'll leave that between you and your conscience.

***"There are very few monsters who warrant the fear we have of them."***

**French Philosopher Andre Gide**

A lot of what you fear disappears once you get started.

Except that creepy guy in Accounts Receivable. Him I worry about.

***"No question is so difficult to answer as that to which the answer is obvious."***

**George Bernard Shaw**

I have no idea what this means, so I guess that means it's obvious.

***"Each generation imagines itself to be more intelligent than the one that went before it and wiser than the one that comes after it."***

**George Orwell**

In your case, of course, this is true. This helps explain why your bosses know nothing and your interns know less.

Which is great except your boss and your direct reports are reading the same quote and agreeing with it.

***"For every man the world is as fresh as it was at the first day, and as full of untold novelties for him who has the eyes to see them."***

**Thomas Henry Huxley**

Which is just a fancy way of saying Mondays aren't all that bad. Get your crack out of bed.

***"Knowledge is of two kinds... we know a subject ourselves, or we know where we can find information upon it...."***

**Samuel Johnson**
**(at least he claims the credit for it)**

This is a constant source of tension with my daughter, Her Serene Highness. Why know how to do something if you have a calculator that will do it for you? Google replaces the need for memorization.

This works great until a power outage, then she nudges the keyboard with her nose and whines like an Irish Setter with an empty dish.

You need both kinds of knowledge if you're not going to be someone's lunch when the Apocalypse comes.

***"He gains everyone's approval who mixes the pleasant with the useful."***

**Roman Poet Horace**

Which is why, despite its environmental credentials, reusable hemp toilet paper will never catch on.

***"The Fool wonders, the Wise Man asks."***

**Benjamin Disraeli**

There is nothing more satisfying than asking a stupid question, only to have everyone else say, "Yeah I was wondering that too."

Nothing, that is, except the stunned look on the face of the vendor who can't answer it.

***"Reading furnishes the mind only with materials of knowledge; it is thinking that makes what we read ours."***

**John Locke**

Reading without talking about it, sharing and putting it into action if it's the right thing to do is simply data collection.

***"Happiness and misery depend not on how high or low down you are, but the direction in which you are tending."***

**Samuel Butler**

Anyone can have a bad day, but it's the general direction… is there light at the end of that tunnel?

Some people are optimists, some are pessimists. For some "the glass is half full." For others, the "glass is half full but it was full when I put it down.. you drank it didn't you, you weasel?"

Misery is optional.

***"Let not sleep fall upon thy eyes 'til thou hast thrice reviewed the transactions of the past day. Where have I turned aside from rectitude? What have I been doing? What have I left undone, which I ought to have done? Begin thus from the first act, and proceed; and in conclusion, at the ill which thou has done, be troubled, and rejoice for the good."***

**Pythagoras**

Remember when the hardest thing Pythagoras asked us to do was solve for the hypotenuse?

***"In Youth we learn, in Age we understand."***

**Marie Von Ebner Eschenbach**

In other words, lighten up on the interns, listen to the old timers.

You've been one and with any luck will become the other… maybe someone will listen to you eventually.

***"Small opportunities are often the beginning of great enterprises."***

**Demosthenes**

Shut up and put the coffee on.

***"The mind is not a hermit's cell, but a place of hospitality and intercourse."***

**Charles Horton Cooley**

1) HR people, relax. He means social intercourse.
2) This means you have to get out there, share your thoughts and network; learn to meet your co workers, go to conferences. Which means,
3) I have to remind you about 1).

***"Neither a man, nor a crowd, nor a nation can be trusted to act humanely or to think sanely under the influence of great fear."***

**Bertrand Russell**

Don't save their performance reviews 'til the end of the year. It creates too much drama.

***"Guard against the prestige of great names; see that your judgments are your own; and do not shrink from disagreement; no trusting without testing."***

**John Emerich Edward Dalbergh Acton**

Okay, I know this book is pretty much full of big words from people with impressive resumes, but it doesn't mean you're supposed to swallow them whole.

Remember - they're famous, but a bigger group of drunks, carousers, hypocrites and stab wound victims has seldom been collected outside a Turmel family reunion.

***"No man, for any considerable period, can wear one face to himself and another to the multitude without finally getting bewildered as to which one is true."***

**Nathaniel Hawthorne**

Before The Duchess leaves the house, she always says, "I have to put my face on." I always ask, "That's the one you're picking?"

My wife doesn't find it funny either (it is, after all, a fine face), but there is a point.

Which face are you choosing to display and how authentic is it?

***"Every now and then go away, have a little relaxation, for when you come back to your work your judgment will be surer. Go some distance away because then the work appears smaller and more of it can be taken in at a glance and a lack of harmony and proportion is more readily seen."***

**Leonardo da Vinci**

When one of the world's great workaholics is telling you to chill, you have a problem.

Start by not answering email on the weekend. Blame the VPN, that always works.

***"Those who dream by day are cognizant of many things that escape those who dream only by night."***

**Edgar Allan Poe**

Of course, unlike Poe, you and I should do that daydreaming without the stuff that shows up in mandatory urine tests.

Check with your HR department to see if Laudanum is still on the list.

***"At times it is folly to hasten, at other times, to delay. The wise do everything in its proper time."***

**Ovid**

I know this one is lacking in specifics, but it's good to have it handy when people start screaming about missed deadlines.

Quoting dead Roman poets is way better than whining, "It'll be done when it's done."

***"Pride attaches undue importance to the superiority of one's status in the eyes of others; And shame is fear of humiliation at one's inferior status in the estimation of others. When one sets his heart on being highly esteemed and achieves such rating, then he is automatically involved in fear of losing his status."***

**Lao Tzu**

I like to hang this just behind me when I call people in for performance reviews. Takes the sting out of a "doesn't meet expectations."

***"Every man is more than just himself; he also represents the unique, the very special and always significant and remarkable point at which the world's phenomena intersect, only once in this way, and never again."***

**Herman Hesse**

This means that, technically, you can't ever make the same hiring mistake again. Doesn't that make you feel better?

***"Do not spoil what you have by desiring what you have not; remember that what you now have was once among the things you only hoped for."***

**Epicurus**

You applied for this management job, remember?

***"The wise man must remember that while he is a descendant of the past, he is a parent of the future."***

**Herbert Spencer**

What he's basically saying is you can't control how you got there but you CAN control the future, a bit.

Spencer obviously never had teenagers. You can't control squat.

***"There is one word that may serve as a rule of practice for all one's life – reciprocity."***

**Confucius**
**(despite what Samuel Johnson claims)**

This is good advice and even if all you do today is look up *reciprocity* your world is already a better place.

You're welcome.

***"'Tis better to do things systematically, since we are only humans, and disorder is our worst enemy."***

**Greek Philosopher Hesiod**

Actually, the neighbor with the annoying Rottweiler is my worst enemy, but no system will help there.

At least a system will help at work.

***"You need chaos in your soul to give birth to a dancing star…."***

**Friedrich Nietzche**

Nietzche was not exactly known as a bundle of laughs and it's hard to imagine him giving birth to a dancing anything, but the idea that from chaos *can* come beautiful things is just a little ray of sunshine don't you think?

***"New opinions are always suspected, and usually opposed without any other reason but because they are not already common."***

**John Locke**

I bring this to you from his essay called, "An Essay Concerning Human Understanding." A more appropriate title I can't imagine.

***"Good intentions will always be pleaded for any assumption of power. There are men in all ages who mean to govern well, but they mean to govern. They promise to be good masters, but they mean to be masters."***

**Daniel Webster**

Whenever I hear about a "flat organization", there are two possible definitions:

1) Someone has made careful, thoughtful decisions to help the top level of an organization communicate better with the front lines for better efficiency.
2) Someone has tried to build an office tower with just a basement and a penthouse.

***"He who is unable to live in society, or who has no need because he is sufficient for himself, must be either a beast or a god."***

**Aristotle**

...and probably works in either IT or finance.

***"The ruler should govern the state as one cooks a small fish – that is don't turn it so often in the pan that it disintegrates…."***

**Lao Tzu**

And manage one's department the same way. Make a decision and get out of the way….

***"Everybody, sooner or later, sits down to a banquet of consequences."***

**Robert Louis Stevenson**

What you say, do and think will eventually catch up to you so best you make it positive and get Karma on your side or you might choke on it. I don't know anyone big enough for that spiritual Heimlich maneuver.

*" The greater danger for most of us lies not in setting our aim too high and falling short, but in setting our aim too low and achieving our mark."*

**Michelangelo di Lodovico Buonarroti Simoni**

If everyone on your team exceeds expectations, do something about those expectations.

If you meet expectations, your boss is a fine judge of talent and doing a terrific job.

***"Instead of saying that man is the creature of circumstance, it would be nearer the mark to say that man is the architect of circumstance."***

**Thomas Carlyle**

This is even more imposing when done with a pompous Scottish brogue. We are the architects of our circumstances, brethren and sistren. What are you building?

***"Strong character is brought out by change, weak ones by permanence."***

**Jean Paul Richter**

The "same old, same old" is fine if the same old really is good.

If you want people to love and buy in to the way you're doing things now, spread the rumor you're about to change it.

***"Science is organized knowledge, Wisdom is organized life."***

**Immanuel Kant**

Knowing is one thing. We KNOW what we're supposed to do. Living it is something else all together.

***"If you wish to appear agreeable in society, you must consent to be taught many things which you know already."***

**Johann Kasper Lavater**

Would it kill you to let someone else be the smartest person in the room once in a while? Smile, nod and say, "good point, thank you."

For some reason The Duchess insisted I put this one in this collection.

***"Deliberate as much as you please, but when you decide it's once and for all...."***

**Publilius Syrus**

Good process people those Romans. Rules, processes, tradition, determination. No surprise the three most successful groups to come out of Italy are the Roman Army, the Catholic Church and the Mafia.

***"The best teacher is the one who suggests rather than dogmatizes, and inspires his listener with the wish to teach himself."***

**Edward Bulwer Lytton**

Nowadays he is known unfairly as one of the worst writers in the English language, but even a blind pig finds an acorn once in a while.

***"If you're going to tell people the truth, make them laugh or they'll kill you."***

**George Bernard Shaw**

Such is the legacy of jesters, comedians and podcast hosts. Don't let the weasels get you down.

Wayne Turmel is a professional writer, speaker, trainer and smart aleck. Originally from a small town in Canada, he has a background as a standup comic, car salesman, corporate trainer and business owner.

He's president of GreatWebMeetings.com as well as the host of one of the Internet's best management podcasts, The Cranky Middle Manager Show™.

Thousands of people around the world have heard him interview the brightest minds in the management field as well as introduce them to historical figures and quotes that challenge, comfort and make them laugh.

Wayne lives in Glen Ellyn, Illinois with The Duchess (Joan), Her Serene Highness (daughter Nora) and Jacky the Wonder Dog.

You can learn more about Wayne and how to have him speak to your group at www.crankymiddlemanager.com.

Managers"?
- What are the changes in technology your kids and competition know about but your managers might not?
- Do you know how 2,000 year old business advice can help the people in your company?
- Are the weasels getting you down?

Wayne Turmel, host of one of the world's most popular management podcasts, **The Cranky Middle Manager Show™**, will bring his unique mix of humor and insight to your group. Whether it's a keynote speech or an interactive break-out session, see how he inspires your group to be their best, meet those goals and have some laughs along the way. Find out why thousands of listeners around the world tune in.

The Cranky Middle Manager Show
http://cmm.thepodcastnetwork.com
www.crankymiddlemanager.com
wayne@crankymiddlemanager.com

## Don't let the weasels get you down!

"Wayne and his show are irreverent, fun, a little crazy and very meaningful – all at the same time. Listen up!"

Marshall Goldsmith,
Author of *What Got You Here Won't Get You There*

"The Cranky Middle Manager Show is one of the best HR Blogs out there."

Inc. Magazine Online

www.ingramcontent.com/pod-product-compliance
Lightning Source LLC
LaVergne TN
LVHW020636100826
845148LV00012B/2208

*9780982037706*